The Big Green Poetry Machine

Defenders Of The Planet

Edited By Jenni Harrison

First published in Great Britain in 2023 by:

Young Writers
Remus House
Coltsfoot Drive
Peterborough
PE2 9BF
Telephone: 01733 890066
Website: www.youngwriters.co.uk

All Rights Reserved
Book Design by Ashley Janson
© Copyright Contributors 2023
Softback ISBN 978-1-80459-607-4

Printed and bound in the UK by BookPrintingUK
Website: www.bookprintinguk.com
YB0545W

FOREWORD

Welcome Reader,

For Young Writers' latest competition The Big Green Poetry Machine, we asked primary school pupils to craft a poem about the world. From nature and environmental issues to exploring their own habitats or those of others around the globe, it provided pupils with the opportunity to share their thoughts and feelings about the world around them.

Here at Young Writers our aim is to encourage creativity in children and to inspire a love of the written word, so it's great to get such an amazing response, with some absolutely fantastic poems. It's important for children to be aware of the world around them and some of the issues we face, but also to celebrate what makes it great! This competition allowed them to express their hopes and fears or simply write about their favourite things. The Big Green Poetry Machine gave them the power of words and the result is a wonderful collection of inspirational and moving poems in a variety of poetic styles.

I'd like to congratulate all the young poets in this anthology; I hope this inspires them to continue with their creative writing.

CONTENTS

Lunt's Heath Primary School, Widnes

Lucas Berry (7)	1
Jasmine Dennett (7)	2
Yuvan Sunil (7)	3
Ewa Godwin (7)	4
Darcey Mitchell (7)	5
George Barrow (7)	6
Carter Dulson (7)	7
Amelie Hasalamaj (7)	8
Pheobe Caswell-Highton (6)	9
Rose Connolly (7)	10
Olivia Williamson (6)	11
Alice Brady Duck (6)	12
Jessica Williamson (6)	13
Norah Rainford-Jones (7)	14
Daisy Gerrard (6)	15
Scarlett Campbell (7)	16
Samuel Doubleday (7)	17
Indi Rae Quinn (6)	18

Middleton Park School, Bridge Of Don

Tami Anna Osofero (7)	19
Migle Gustaityte (7)	20
Matilda Thackeray (7)	21
Maya Pitera (7)	22
Emily du Plessis (7)	23
Matilda Robb (7)	24
River Young (7)	25
Euan Boyle (7)	26
Amy Purvis (6)	27

Robert Fitzroy Academy, Croydon

Mila Zaniewska (8)	28
Malachi Thomas (9)	30
Josiah Gordon (9)	31
Eloise Flemmings (8)	32
Poppy Broame (10)	34
Anaïs-Elise Esimaje (8)	35
Ava Francis-Williams (8)	36
Ana Biatriz Rodrigues (9)	37
Violet Harman (8)	38
Jayden Lovegrove Rogers (9)	39
Allegra Henriques (9)	40
Laszlo Szebeni Rees (10)	41

St Clare's RC Primary School, Middlesbrough

Poppy Gair (8)	42
Matthew Donnelly (8)	43
Eleanor Ferguson (7)	44
Isaac Bowes (8)	45
Megan Bodiong (8)	46
Ella-Grace Dobson (7)	47
Julia Pecynska (7)	48
Eleanor Caswell (8)	49
Emilie Ewbank (7)	50
Nancy Connolly (7)	51
George Gillespie (7)	52
Joseph Battensby (7)	53
Seb Howe (8)	54
Elias Beaumont (7)	55
Philip Sikora (8)	56
Jakob Donnelly (8)	57
Connor Crosby (7)	58
Jacob Douglas (7)	59

Parker Colligan (7)	60
Joshua Longstaff (7)	61
Annabelle Dalton (8)	62
Elizabeth Brown (7)	63
Madelaine Robinson (7)	64
Maya Pecynska (7)	65
Joseph Fovargue (7)	66
Freddie Steel (8)	67
Noah Brown (7)	68
Olly Varey (7)	69
Elijah Boldison (8)	70
Jake Smith (8)	71

St Joseph's RC Primary School, London

Olivia Cipriano (10)	72
Saviour Higgans (7)	74
Nellie Bloomfield (8)	76
Vicente Barardo Ribeiro (8)	77
Sofia Rizzato (10)	78
Martha Lamb (10)	79
Sofia Marchuk (8)	80
Alyssa Yap (11)	81
Sapphire Awel Dinesen (8)	82
Sienna Fouad (8)	83
Sofía Zuleta-Casal (7)	84
Tom Koka (9)	85
Cece Stacey (10)	86
Edward Dallari (8)	87
Kali Dolcy-Campbell (8)	88
Alexandra Gajewska (10)	89
Mariana Silva (11)	90
Benedetta Rossi (10)	91
Penny Miller (8)	92
Eric Flynn Vicari (8)	93
Julieta Martin-Simo (9)	94
Pablo Cava (8)	95
Maria Bianqui (10)	96
Patrick Trainor (6)	97
Elena Guinea (7)	98
Phoebe Spiteri Hammer (6)	99
Anna Rizzato (10)	100
Mariana Sousa (8)	101
Edie O'Brien (8)	102
Sophia Garrido Franco (8)	103
Arabella Kojm Thompson (7)	104
Tita Mondedeu (6)	105
Sesinna Zerezghi (7)	106
Kai Man (10)	107
Ella Cali Gravier (7)	108
Cecilia Bailey (7)	109
Tomas Sanchez Roba (6)	110
Joel Fosu-Simpson (7)	111
Isabella Lopez Alban (6)	112
Christian Rafferty (6)	113
Leo Dallari (5)	114
Ollie Henriot (7)	115
Bella Pagnello Symmons (8)	116
Carmen Bianqui (6)	117
Teresa Martin (5)	118
Hans Lau (6)	119
Harry Leslie (7)	120

St Thomas' Primary School, Riddrie

Maya Tworzydlo (8)	121
Lucy Graham (8)	122
Xuxi He (9)	123
Tianna Baird (8)	124
Jouri Alhamadani (8)	125
Milly Clelland (8)	126
Louis Millican (9)	127
Rebecca Winter (8)	128
Macy Bannerman (8)	129
Aaron Murray (8)	130
Sienna Scott (8)	131
Ryan McEwan (8)	132
Aiden Cawley (8)	133
Layla McConnell (8)	134
Zac Brown (8)	135
Kirah O'Connor (8)	136
Jessica Little (8)	137
Jessica Kane (8)	138

What Is It?

Most dangerous animal from the weasel family.
It is beautiful.
It is vicious.
It lives in cold climates.
It is furry.
It has sharp teeth and claws.
It is a scavenger and a predator at the same time.
Wolves, bears, cougars and golden eagles are its enemies.
I can be brown and black.
It has a great sense of smell.
There is a superhero named after it.
What is it?

Answer: Wolverine.

Lucas Berry (7)
Lunt's Heath Primary School, Widnes

Forests And Nature Are Very Important

I live in the beautiful nature.
I'm very important to the environment.
I am something that sits on top of roots.
Lots of flowers hang off me.
I'm surrounded by all different bushes.
I give oxygen to the world.
Birds fly up to me and make small nests.
My home sometimes is in the park.
Lots of children climb on me.
I'm green and brown.
I'm found in every single country.

Jasmine Dennett (7)
Lunt's Heath Primary School, Widnes

Wildfire

W hen you're camping,
I f you put a bottle near a bunch of leaves, there will be a fire.
L et a parent or a fireman,
D on't act back.
F irst, cover your nose and mouth and get in a vehicle.
I f your vehicle has no fuel, call 999.
R apidly go somewhere safe.
E ventually relax at home.

Yuvan Sunil (7)
Lunt's Heath Primary School, Widnes

Arctic Foxes

A rctic foxes live in the Arctic.
R un on the snow.
C hases some animals.
T ake food.
I n case you see one, they might hurt you.
C hases fish.

F ast at running.
O n ice they live.
X -rays show I have four legs.
E at fish.
S ave them.

Ewa Godwin (7)
Lunt's Heath Primary School, Widnes

Wildlife

W ildlife is very cool.
I t's about animals, I care as some don't care.
L ogs, trees, it's the animals' homes,
D o you chop trees? Well don't.
L ots of animals
I f you save the Earth.
F lowers and trees
E veryone save the world.

Darcey Mitchell (7)
Lunt's Heath Primary School, Widnes

What Am I?

I'm big and mostly green,
I have lots of wildlife.
If you walk in it,
You'll be calm.
You can hear the birds tweeting in there.
There is a stream in some of it.
Some people take a walk in it.
It has giant trees in it.
I have nature all around me.
What am I?

George Barrow (7)
Lunt's Heath Primary School, Widnes

The Earth

What am I?
I am green and round.
I have water and I have an imaginary line around me.
I have lots of oceans and countries.
I have got wildlife and human beings.
I have lots of species of animals.

Carter Dulson (7)
Lunt's Heath Primary School, Widnes

Forest

F lowers grow gracefully.
O xygen comes from me.
R oots grow below me.
E njoy walking above me.
S ave our world.
T rees grow all around as you can see.

Amelie Hasalamaj (7)
Lunt's Heath Primary School, Widnes

The Forest

N ature is loving
A nimals are living
T rees are growing
U nderground, there are bugs
R unning bugs are nice
E verywhere people care about animals.

Pheobe Caswell-Highton (6)
Lunt's Heath Primary School, Widnes

The Sea

It's blue everywhere.
Lots of fish.
Some coral.
Tons of hammerheads.
Tons of whales.
Tons of jellyfish.
Some sharks.
Big and small dogfish.
Small stingrays.

Rose Connolly (7)
Lunt's Heath Primary School, Widnes

Earth Is Our Planet

E lephants are on our planet
A nimals that we look after
R ocks that animals live in
T rees that are really tall
H omes that are warm for you.

Olivia Williamson (6)
Lunt's Heath Primary School, Widnes

Nature

N ature is a beautiful place
A nimals live there.
T rees are there.
U nusual places are there.
R espect animals.
E ggs are chicks.

Alice Brady Duck (6)
Lunt's Heath Primary School, Widnes

Plants

P erfect plants grow
L ight plants have colour
A nimals have habitats
N atural area
T rees to grow
S ome get watered.

Jessica Williamson (6)
Lunt's Heath Primary School, Widnes

Nature

N ature was naturally there
A nimals live there
T rees are there
U nusual places are there
R elaxing
E co-friendly.

Norah Rainford-Jones (7)
Lunt's Heath Primary School, Widnes

Nature

N ature.
A nimals live in habitats.
T rees are tall.
U nusual home for animals.
R ough grasses
E pic animals.

Daisy Gerrard (6)
Lunt's Heath Primary School, Widnes

The Ocean

O pen water.
C an go to the water.
E verywhere
A nd go to the beach.
N o littering.

Scarlett Campbell (7)
Lunt's Heath Primary School, Widnes

The Ocean

The ocean has sharks and catfish
The ocean has seaweed
The ocean has coral and different fish
And whales and sharks.

Samuel Doubleday (7)
Lunt's Heath Primary School, Widnes

What Am I?

It is big
It is round
There are police
There are animals
It has oceans.

Indi Rae Quinn (6)
Lunt's Heath Primary School, Widnes

Nature And Rubbish And Pollution

O ur planet can't have rubbish because the animals will die,
U nder the sea the fish are dying because of plastic and rubbish.
R ubbish is not good for the environment, it makes places dirty and bad,

P ollution is not good for the environment.
L itter is very bad, don't litter.
A lways put litter in the bin, it always helps.
N ature needs to be safe for wild animals and little creatures.
E nvironment is full of litter right now.
T he animals can't breathe because of rubbish and pollution.

Tami Anna Osofero (7)
Middleton Park School, Bridge Of Don

The Big Green

O ur planet is unhealthy
U p in the sky, there's rubbish and birds are flying too
R ainforests are in serious danger.

P eople have to look after the Earth
L itter people are very bad
A round the Earth
N ever put litter on the ground
E veryone needs to learn to recycle
T urtles.

Migle Gustaityte (7)
Middleton Park School, Bridge Of Don

Our Planet

O ur planet is in danger.
U p in the air, there's rubbish too.
R ecycle more and more.

P lease help wildlife.
L ittering is bad too.
A lot of rubbish is in the sea.
N ature needs help.
E xtra litter is everywhere.
T ropical forests need help too.

Matilda Thackeray (7)
Middleton Park School, Bridge Of Don

The Big Green

O ur planet is unhealthy,
U p in the sky, there's rubbish too.
R ainforests are in danger.

P eople shall recycle their rubbish,
L ive safely.
A ll others must be safe,
N o rubbish shall be left.
E at healthily,
T hey have to help.

Maya Pitera (7)
Middleton Park School, Bridge Of Don

Our Planet

O ur planet is in danger
U nderstand rainforests too
R escue our planet please

P ollution is in our world
L ittering is very bad
A nimals are endangering
N ature needs big help
E xtinct animals are becoming
T ry and help our planet.

Emily du Plessis (7)
Middleton Park School, Bridge Of Don

Animals

A nimals are cute and small.
N ature is a good place for animals.
I t's good for animals to live.
M ice are small, so be careful.
A nimals are cute.
L ong animals are cool.
S eeing animals is cool.

Matilda Robb (7)
Middleton Park School, Bridge Of Don

Cute Earth

A nts in the sunny woods
N ature is good for you
I ce is melting, can you help?
M ountains
A nteaters are cool
L illies are good
S nakes are scary.

River Young (7)
Middleton Park School, Bridge Of Don

Pokémon

P okémon are cool.
O pponents are strong
K orrina is a trainer
É ternatus is a legendary
M eowth
O ctolock
N o!

Euan Boyle (7)
Middleton Park School, Bridge Of Don

Jungle

J umping things
U nder trees
N ature is good
G rowing trees
L akes
E lephants.

Amy Purvis (6)
Middleton Park School, Bridge Of Don

The Worst World In History

Long ago the world was fair, clear air and kind share.
It's when people shared the world with nature,
Wildlife and more, but now made them poor.
Humans have taken over the world!
Our carbon footprint affects the Earth, pollutes the sky, litters the streets.
Some people try to help but nothing works, so they weep.
Not enough people try, that's the reason why.
Everyone should step up to save their home,
To make it clean as an ice cream cone.
Help our planet, oh please, oh please,
Corals die, ice caps melt, animals become extinct and polluted sky.
Our planet is perfect no more, it's the worst world in history.
But we change that if you follow rules and listen and you will stop this evil turn.
Switch off lights after use, honestly, there's no excuse.

Put your rubbish in the right bin, used by you and your kin.
Use renewable energy, it's easy as a stick of celery.
We should save the world.
It should be turned into something good and clean.
It shouldn't be dirty and mean.
In the worst world in history.

Mila Zaniewska (8)
Robert Fitzroy Academy, Croydon

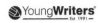

The Tree's Cry

Dear humans,
Climate change has made me really mad,
I just hope you'd help the environment,
It's really bad.
You cut down one tree, then come for another,
I wish you would just listen to me, 'cause I'm a nature lover.

Animals lose their homes,
The world will become a wasteland.
If we don't save and protect, plus aid Mother Nature,
There will be a ton of issues and these ones we can't solve with tissues.

You see, all the animals depend on one another,
So please tell this to your sister and your brother.
Plastic pollutes the seas,
So you won't be able to go to the sea as you please.

What we should do to make a better Earth
Is be kind to our rainforest because recycling is fun.

Malachi Thomas (9)
Robert Fitzroy Academy, Croydon

Woah, What A Dream!

Whoa! What a dream I had,
Where I was in Candyland and I swam with marshmallows and after we danced.
What a dream I had!
I had a dream where I was in a spooky, haunted house with a scary vampire.
Whoa, what a dream I had.
I had the best dream ever,
I was in a twisted world,
The floor was cracked,
Trains were twisted.
Whoa, what a dream that was.
I had a dream where the nightmare monster came to destroy all of my good dreams,
But I knew it was a dream and woke up.
I said, "Oh no, my good dreams are gone."
But I thought about the good dreams
And it came back to my mind and I slept the night away.

Josiah Gordon (9)
Robert Fitzroy Academy, Croydon

Animals In The World

Animals of the world, big and small
From the deep vast sea to the bright soft shore
Plants live too, so we must care
Love each other everywhere.

Animals that hop
Animals that run
We all live together, all as one
Animals and nature, God's design
We must make sure that they're happy and healthy
And that's fine.

Now owls hoot
Lions roar
Snakes hiss and many more!

I love nature, I love dogs
I love animals and so much more!
Now we must care for people, animals and plants too

So let's make a world where there is peace and love
I love you world, all in one.

Eloise Flemmings (8)
Robert Fitzroy Academy, Croydon

Nature, Oh Nature

Nature, oh nature,
What a wonderful thing it can be,
Just not seeing the animals flee.
From green leaves to beautiful flowers
And being far away from the city towers.
It is a love for all, I much prefer it than the mall.
It gives me freedom,
Like I have my own kingdom.
Those sticks and stones,
Won't break my bones.
Being there is the best,
There I always feel like I'm on a quest.
Nature, oh nature,
You're something all should adore.

Poppy Broame (10)
Robert Fitzroy Academy, Croydon

The Unbreakable Temple

This unusual, tall island,
Stands proudly above the warm, wavy water.

Birds circle and flap
Around the leafy trees.
Suddenly it shone bright like a diamond.

Far, far away, stands a magnificent golden temple,
With East Island statues on the top.
The statues have golden, yellow eyes
That shine bright like a diamond.

This island seemed uncovered,
The enormous rocky statues look like big statues,
That shine bright like a diamond.

Anaïs-Elise Esimaje (8)
Robert Fitzroy Academy, Croydon

Nature, Nature

Nature, nature everywhere, beware
As furious danger is in the air
Earth is no longer safe for you
You must show us humans what's fair
Just like the mayor
The environment is changing for the worst
Climate is just the worst
Nobody recycles, please just teach them a lesson
Pollution is getting badder than bad
I thoroughly appreciate you haven't hurt any of us, Mother Nature
Without you, our dreams would cease to exist
We would be extinct.

Ava Francis-Williams (8)
Robert Fitzroy Academy, Croydon

Environment

Environment, environment, follow me,
Make a wish and your mind will be.
Now I have a song,
My wish is this green, green grass.
Blue, blue sky,
Be ready for a party on the day that I come.
I'm coming today to hear your beautiful voices,
Don't worry, I'm going to be there.
So don't be shy and I'll be proud.
Now it's time to play.
Plays inside, plays outside,
Let's do it, come on y'all, alright!

Ana Biatriz Rodrigues (9)
Robert Fitzroy Academy, Croydon

Fly Butterfly

To egg, caterpillar, cocoon, a butterfly is here
Fly high, little butterfly
Be a butterfly
Eat like them, speak like them, drink like them
Play like a butterfly
Sit like them
Rain is falling while the sun is shining
While the leaves are blowing and the bees are humming
The trees are growing, the birds are knowing
It's time to start going south while the rainbows are smiling.

Violet Harman (8)
Robert Fitzroy Academy, Croydon

Space

Space is big
Bigger than Earth
You never knew
That space is all black
You will not survive in outer space
Space is more than you think
It goes on for miles
You will fly, fly away
So don't try to
If you do, just jump
You will fly for miles
So just don't
In space it is all black
And won't see for miles and miles
It is space for you okay.

Jayden Lovegrove Rogers (9)
Robert Fitzroy Academy, Croydon

The Battle Of The Seasons

Haiku Poetry

Winter comes with fear,
Biting bleak wind stings your soul,
Eternal, cold, dark.

At last, spring is here,
Rain falls and petals open,
A new beginning.

Summer is here - joy,
Long days, warm nights - happiness,
Orange hues arrive.

Colours warm the trees,
Before they start to drift down,
Autumn fades away...

Allegra Henriques (9)
Robert Fitzroy Academy, Croydon

No Day's The Same

Leaves swish,
Knees lift,
Wings flap,
Fins snap,
You pollute but don't know what you dilute,
Where people lie and die,
Listen closely to the life we're creating,
Where no day is the same in the making.

Laszlo Szebeni Rees (10)
Robert Fitzroy Academy, Croydon

The Environment

E verywhere you look, there is sadness all around
N ature is dying because of us
V iruses are spreading all around
I nsects and creatures are lifeless
R ivers are getting full of plastic
O n each day, we throw litter everywhere
N o please, everybody stop hurting God's world
M ost people could help if they were willing
E veryone needs to stop hurting the world
N ow let's work as a team
T ogether we can make a change.

Poppy Gair (8)
St Clare's RC Primary School, Middlesbrough

Helpless Nature

N ature is dying - no one is helping. We all need to start to help.
A re you noticing the harm you're doing? All the trees are dying, we need to start helping
T rees lying lifeless on the ground, start helping
U p in the sky, birds are escaping from the dark shadow of death
R ivers are getting filled with plastic waste
E verywhere you look, nature is being killed by all the smoke from factories, help the Earth.

Matthew Donnelly (8)
St Clare's RC Primary School, Middlesbrough

Don't Disappoint Our Earth!

P ollution is killing
O ur Earth's disappointed
L ifeless animals are crying in pain for help
L udicrous people are spreading toxic chemicals
U nknown people are dying as well because people are killing
T rees are suffocating
I t is your job to help
O utside is dying
N o one is helping, save the wonderful Earth!

Eleanor Ferguson (7)
St Clare's RC Primary School, Middlesbrough

Smoke

S moke is polluting the Earth and invading people's lungs
M any animals are suffocating and need your help
O ther living things are crying for help
K eep the animals and other living things safe from pollution
E veryone needs to stop the spread of this terrible disease.

Isaac Bowes (8)
St Clare's RC Primary School, Middlesbrough

Earth's Dying

N ature is dying from the cloud of death
A nimals are tortured from the black blanket of death
T rees are suffocating and burning
U p in the air, birds are falling to the death
R ivers are getting dirty from the pollution
E ventually the world will be destroyed.

Megan Bodiong (8)
St Clare's RC Primary School, Middlesbrough

The World Dying, Save It

Smoke is spreading so we need to stop
Or our animals are going to die
Many trees are burning down
We can't breathe without them
Our beautiful world is full of pollution
It is starting to disappear
Killing the things we need most
Everyone needs something to help
Save our world!

Ella-Grace Dobson (7)
St Clare's RC Primary School, Middlesbrough

Plastic

P lastic is horrible, dirty and smashed
L ots of towns have been trodden on
A ll of the rubbish is in the ocean
S inking plastic is hurting the sea creatures
T he Earth is hurting
I llnesses are spreading
C reatures are running, suffocating.

Julia Pecynska (7)
St Clare's RC Primary School, Middlesbrough

Save The Earth!

N ature needs your help
A nimals are getting abused by us
T orture is harming a lot of innocent animals
U ntil people end pollution, we're all in danger
R espect nature's land of creatures
E verywhere you look is all burnt down and gloomy.

Eleanor Caswell (8)
St Clare's RC Primary School, Middlesbrough

Save The Earth!

S ave our polluted environment
M any animals and people are dying and suffocating because of the big black cloud of death
O n Earth, the wildlife is dying all because of the smoke
K eep saving the beautiful world we live on
E very little helps. What am I?

Emilie Ewbank (7)
St Clare's RC Primary School, Middlesbrough

Suffocating Smoke

S ome people are suffocating and some people are lifeless
M ighty trees are lifeless but are trying to survive
O ther living things are lying lifeless on the ground
K illed by the grey shadow of death
E verything is dying, so we need to stop the smoke.

Nancy Connolly (7)
St Clare's RC Primary School, Middlesbrough

Help Earth

I get thrown on the sticky ground
I'm full of pollution most days
People throw me in the sea, torturing sea animals.
Get me out!
Germs everywhere, surrounding the environment
I'm disappointed, just recycle me.
What am I?

Answer: Plastic.

George Gillespie (7)
St Clare's RC Primary School, Middlesbrough

Save Our World

S moke is killing nature and the world.
M any people are dying from the dusty, dirty pollution.
O nly we can protect the Earth.
K eeping the planet safe from the terrible smoke.
E ventually it will destroy the planet and animals.
Save our world!

Joseph Battensby (7)
St Clare's RC Primary School, Middlesbrough

The Tortured Turtle

I float around with plastic choking me
I think infected is food
Eating too much plastic can kill me
I should live in clear blue water but instead
I live in polluted plastic water
I feel tortured in my home
What am I?

Answer: A turtle.

Seb Howe (8)
St Clare's RC Primary School, Middlesbrough

About The Smoke

S moke is spreading and killing beautiful nature
M ore and more smoke is polluting our lovely world
O ften it is a dark shadow of death
K illing more and more nature and nothing is left
E veryone and everything is dying, we must stop!

Elias Beaumont (7)
St Clare's RC Primary School, Middlesbrough

Help, Smoke!

S moke is killing the world, slowly and steadily.
M ore and more, nature is dying from the evil smoke.
O ther animals are dying in the world.
K illing the animals is the worst thing ever.
E nd this now, please help the world!

Philip Sikora (8)
St Clare's RC Primary School, Middlesbrough

Can I Help The Environment?

S moke is all around, it's everywhere, you can trap it
M ost things are breathing in oxygen
O ur trees and plants are dying out
K eep recycling, let's keep our planet safe
E veryone needs to help save the Earth.

Jakob Donnelly (8)
St Clare's RC Primary School, Middlesbrough

What Am I?

I am a beautiful sea creature
I move extremely slow
I think dull plastic is delicious food
I am choking on the rubbish you wash out to sea
My shell might be hard but my heart isn't
What am I?

Answer: A sea turtle.

Connor Crosby (7)
St Clare's RC Primary School, Middlesbrough

Save Our Nature

S ave our nature and save our world
M any animals are dying, our world is full of litter
O nly we can make change
K eep animals safe from the pollution
E ventually animals will become extinct, save our world!

Jacob Douglas (7)
St Clare's RC Primary School, Middlesbrough

Save The World

I am scrumpled up and shot in the air
I am carelessly floating along the streets
I pollute the seas and rivers, torturing innocent animals
My home is the black hole that you can call a bin.
What am I?

Answer: Litter.

Parker Colligan (7)
St Clare's RC Primary School, Middlesbrough

Don't Throw Rubbish!

You think I belong in a dirty bin
I get trodden over and it hurts
I am an unwashed and smelly and disturbing
I am dirty and animals eat me
I am worthless and no one knows about me
What am I?

Answer: Litter.

Joshua Longstaff (7)
St Clare's RC Primary School, Middlesbrough

Smoke

S ee the animals dying with fear
M ost of them suffocating and hiding
O h save the animals, save the animals
K illed by the dark grey shadow death
E ventually the world will become a better place.

Annabelle Dalton (8)
St Clare's RC Primary School, Middlesbrough

The Choking Earth

Continents like Antarctica are hot instead of cold
Look around you, everything is dying
It is killing the Earth
Many fish are dying
Animals are dying
Trees are dying
Everything is dying
Little things are dying.

Elizabeth Brown (7)
St Clare's RC Primary School, Middlesbrough

The Ruined World

I am a grey shadow of death.
I choke animals.
You breathe me in and out without you knowing.
People create me in awful factories.
I look fearless but I am not.
What am I?

Answer: Smoke.

Madelaine Robinson (7)
St Clare's RC Primary School, Middlesbrough

Smoke

S ome animals breathe in the smoke
M ost animals die from suffocating
O ther living things are disappearing
K eep looking after the environment
E veryone needs to save the world.

Maya Pecynska (7)
St Clare's RC Primary School, Middlesbrough

Don't Ruin Our Beautiful World

I am a great big shadow of everlasting death
I choke animals and kill trees
I fill your lungs every day
You breathe me in and out without even knowing.
What am I?

Answer: Smoke.

Joseph Fovargue (7)
St Clare's RC Primary School, Middlesbrough

The Earth

I am a big black shadow of death, floating in the air.
I shoot out of a dirty factory.
Trees are suffocating all around me.
You breathe me in.
What am I?

Answer: Smoke.

Freddie Steel (8)
St Clare's RC Primary School, Middlesbrough

Rubbish

You think I belong on the floor
I am scrumpled up on the floor
Animals are eating me and then choking on me
I love being in the bin
The disgusting smelly bin is where I belong.

Noah Brown (7)
St Clare's RC Primary School, Middlesbrough

Save The Nature

I am a sea creature
I swim with plastic around my neck
Every day I choke and sink further down
Every day I swim around,
Suffocating with all the plastic surrounding me.

Olly Varey (7)
St Clare's RC Primary School, Middlesbrough

Our World Is Important So Save It

H elping our planet will make our world a better place
E very living thing is choking
L et our world live
P eople, save our nature.

Elijah Boldison (8)
St Clare's RC Primary School, Middlesbrough

Do You Know What I Am?

I am fearless.
I am surrounded by plastic pollution.
I am scared of choking on the plastic.
I am strangled every day.
What am I?

Jake Smith (8)
St Clare's RC Primary School, Middlesbrough

As The Rustling Leaves

As the rustling leaves touch my feet,
I breathe the grey smoke that I also eat,
My brown trunk,
My long arms,
My emerald hair,
This is me, a tree!

As the rustling leaves,
Crunch, snap,
I see the men who chop me down,
This is our world, this is our future,
But as a tree, I'm tall and see much more,
Than you could ever see,
They knock down my friends and come back,
With golden coins which they love and adore,
More than me.

As the rustling leaves,
Turn green,
Just like me,
I realise it's summer,
Spring, well it could be,

I give humans air.
Well they return the favour,
But it's a darker colour,
You might think my life's full of glee,
But I see things I wish to never see,
Like water bottles, garbage, plastic,
It's all clumping up my home.

Please stop!
Remember this is our world,
This is our future,
Help me thrive,
I beg you, please!

Olivia Cipriano (10)
St Joseph's RC Primary School, London

Animals Made Extinct

Since the Earth's been turning
Nature's taken control
Since God created humans
And science - the big black hole
We had a beautiful planet
With beautiful animals and plants
But humans decided to ruin
The beauty in their path
Forests have been destroyed
And animals hunted for games
We caused animal extinctions
And these are some of their names,

The Baiji white dolphin from China
They could grow up to 8 feet long
The passenger pigeon from North America
We will no longer hear its song,

The Tasmanian tiger from Australia
With a 2-metre-long tail
The dodo bird who was flightless
That didn't end very well

The black West African rhino
Who only ate plants and thorns
Mankind made them extinct too
Just to get hold of their horns,

Every living creature
No matter how big or small
Deserves a place on our planet
Because the Earth is for us all.

Saviour Higgans (7)
St Joseph's RC Primary School, London

The World

Plants, plants, grow all around,
Look after the environment.
We were made to look after the world,
This is our time to shine.
Every rubbish piece you pick up is a help,
You have to help us save the planet.
Plant new seeds for all of the animals,
Every seed you plant is a change.
Don't put plastic in the ocean,
Make new homes for animals every day.
Each and every day, nature disappears,
Help all of the snails, slugs and worms live.
Reuse plastic bags every day,
You will help us live by planting seeds.
Help us save the world,
Give animals food to live.

Nellie Bloomfield (8)
St Joseph's RC Primary School, London

Stop Chopping Trees!

Stop chopping trees,
From when I was a seed to become a huge tree.
Then when there are no trees, no oxygen, no leaves,
Everyone will be extinct.
Jumping jaguars, slimy snakes and even humans will be dead.
No trees, no oxygen,
No oxygen, no air,
No air, no life,
No life, extinction!

Stop chopping trees,
Don't make us die,
Climate change is bad, it causes pollution!
Our Earth will be grey,
Make renewable energy.
Recycle plastic and elastics,
That's my dream, a world without being mean.

Vicente Barardo Ribeiro (8)
St Joseph's RC Primary School, London

The Four Seasons

Spring is a season of life and growing,
Birth, flowing and sowing,
Fresh plants, new animals,
Let's save nature.

Summer is a season of heat and sun,
Sun, shining and glowing,
Providing the Earth with energy,
Let's save the sun!

Autumn is a season of leaves and trees,
Leaves covering the ground,
Trees provide us with life,
Let's save the trees!

Winter is a season of cold and dying,
Snow falls down and down,
Smothering the Earth,
Let's save it all!

Sofia Rizzato (10)
St Joseph's RC Primary School, London

Save The Seas

The ocean is full of amazing things,
So why should we destroy it?
Vibrant coral reefs and incredible creatures,
So save the seas, save them.

Wonders beyond imaginable,
So don't throw your waste away,
'Cause it will end up on the bay.
Dolphins, fish, seahorses,
And all living things are a part of it all.

So the last thing I'm going to say,
Is do you really want plastic bags,
Wrapped around turtle's necks?
Fish, trapped by a can?
No! So save the seas! Save them!

Martha Lamb (10)
St Joseph's RC Primary School, London

My Planet Is My Soul

My planet is my soul,
Some people need to control
How they care for the Earth,
Because we are making a curse.
Our planet is alive, just like we are,
Because we are giving Earth a big scar,
To treat the Earth better,
We could act kinder and smarter.
We won't chop down trees,
Help me to care for the Earth, oh please!
We need to save water,
If we don't do these things, then we might become poorer,
When you read this poem just always remember,
My planet is my soul!

Sofia Marchuk (8)
St Joseph's RC Primary School, London

I Dream

I dream that I am not alone in this forest
And my tree friends are here with me
That they were never brutally cut down
And I'm not a lonely tree.

I dream all the animals would come back
And bring colourful life to this place
That they could sing their sweet melodies
And bring a smile to my face.

But of course, here I am all alone
With nobody to cheer me up
No one to guide the way for me
My friends' departure was just too abrupt.

Alyssa Yap (11)
St Joseph's RC Primary School, London

The Environment

E arth is our home, so why are we destroying it?
N o animal or human should live in this condition
V aluable Earth, we're treating so badly
I f you look around you
R ealise that you're hurting the Earth
O bject to this destruction
N ature is important
M ake the world a better place
E ven the smallest help will change the world
N ow I hope you listened
T ake my advice.

Sapphire Awel Dinesen (8)
St Joseph's RC Primary School, London

The Tree Of LIfe

The tree I see is full of love, like a dove
I feel so lonely,
I don't know how,
I need a friend, especially for me
I walk and talk to the sky,
But there is no reply
But finally I come upon a great tree!
I carry on talking and suddenly my wish became true,
Standing next to me was a bird that I never saw
As I gazed at it in awe
It was brilliant, colourful, powerful and more,
I finally had a friend as we happily walked home.

Sienna Fouad (8)
St Joseph's RC Primary School, London

Our Planet Earth

Our planet Earth is suffering
And we must do something about it
Animals are dying and our air quality is declining
Our seas are full of plastic
This is not fantastic
We live in a world full of pollution
We have to find a solution
Let's recycle more and focus on the chore
The rainforests are dying by cutting down trees
Please stop this now, this is a plea
If we want a future that's bright
We must put up a fight.

Sofía Zuleta-Casal (7)
St Joseph's RC Primary School, London

Our World

The world was once an island
With old creatures alive
But then it fell apart and now
Our only hope is a bee hive
Tech is now a thing
With lots of clicking and tapping
And instead of using paper
They use phones for mapping
Now they use paper and cut down trees
And at beaches, you're just polluting the seas
The world was once an island
With creatures alive
But now, it's all going to die.

Tom Koka (9)
St Joseph's RC Primary School, London

Our Planet

If there's air,
We can go anywhere.
We can go to the park,
And hear the dogs bark.
We can watch the swaying trees,
And the buzzing bees.
We can sit by the flowers,
And pass away the hours.
We can smell the grass,
When the lawnmowers pass.
We can see the birds fly,
Up high in the sky.
But something for sure,
This will all be no more,
If we don't save our beautiful planet.

Cece Stacey (10)
St Joseph's RC Primary School, London

Save Our Planet

Let's not chop trees or ruin nature
I like to recycle
When it's a plant's lifecycle
We're like nature
That grows up too tall
They try to call
The people chopping and ruining the trees
Let's not chop trees or ruin nature
Let's turn it around
And don't do it all
All I see are trees falling down
With makes animals pain
And nature angry
The same to the trees.

Edward Dallari (8)
St Joseph's RC Primary School, London

Air Pollution

Observe the traffic pollution,
Where is its solution?
I see in my own neighbourhood this sight,
It's not a matter to be taken light.

I see the leaves and trees crying,
And the burnt fallen leaves lying.
I wish that it would stop soon,
Otherwise, we'll have to take refuge on the moon.
Plant trees and take care of them,
So that our lives don't go in vain.

Kali Dolcy-Campbell (8)
St Joseph's RC Primary School, London

Seasons, Seasons!

Spring is first, filled with rain
This season is calm without any pain.
Second is summer, made with light,
It's so warm, it's really too bright!
Third is autumn, colourful trees,
When it's time, they'll make a bunch of leaves!
Last is winter, so much snow!
It makes the sky glow!
That's the end of the poem of seasons,
Love them all because of their reasons!

Alexandra Gajewska (10)
St Joseph's RC Primary School, London

Deforestation

This cause can affect our trees,
The trees that bring us life and air,
Without the trees, the world is nothing,
How could you survive without them?

Those proud trees standing like soldiers,
Protecting us from death,
How could you cut down these marvellous trees?
The ones that bring you life,
If you care so much about our planet,
Stop the deforestation occurring.

Mariana Silva (11)
St Joseph's RC Primary School, London

My Amazon World

The Amazon, wide and big,
On a map seems as big as a twig.
When trees are chopped down,
What is left is the bare ground.

We need to help it grow,
Or then it will soon go.
Give it so much care,
Or it will soon disappear in thin air.

So let's look after it,
Let it grow nice and big!
This is our Earth,
Make it grow and grow!

Benedetta Rossi (10)
St Joseph's RC Primary School, London

Earth

Earth, Earth
Glaciers melting fast
Our planet to last
Just say no to beef
Save our coral reef
Plant-based is the way
For the Earth to see a brighter day
Earth, Earth
Plastics fill the ocean blue
What are we supposed to do?
Pick up plastic here and there
Beautiful planet everywhere
Earth, Earth
It's time to act, no looking back.

Penny Miller (8)
St Joseph's RC Primary School, London

Think

Think about those poor, poor sloths,
Think about these insects like moths.
Think about cheetahs who cannot find,
Their food they will only have in their mind.
Think about monkeys who swing,
Think about bee hives in there, stay away from bees, they can sting.
So please don't chop this lovely tree,
To all of these animals, it's family.

Eric Flynn Vicari (8)
St Joseph's RC Primary School, London

Our Planet

O ur planet is for caring.
U niverse is our place.
R ecycle the most you can.

P aper is from trees, don't waste it.
L ove and care to our world.
A lways follow the nature.
N ever give up on it.
E ncourage everybody to recycle.
T ry to recycle the most you can for our planet.

Julieta Martin-Simo (9)
St Joseph's RC Primary School, London

Jaguars Hunt

There's nothing like a jaguar who tries to find his prey
A grey koala whose great banana got stolen by a monkey
He jumps and swirls merrily and jumps around
Through the beautiful Amazon forest
There's nothing like a jaguar who hunts around the wood
Birds scream, owls howl all around the wood
They fly and cry without a trace left behind.

Pablo Cava (8)
St Joseph's RC Primary School, London

Autumn, Beautiful Autumn

Your green leaves,
They're falling from the trees!
Now they're yellow,
Red and brown.
It's really unknown!
Sometimes I think,
That I'm on the brink,
Of the poor summer,
Now it is cold,
And leaves are gold,
Oh my beautiful autumn,
Return summer,
Or I will hit you like a drummer.

Maria Bianqui (10)
St Joseph's RC Primary School, London

I'm An Ancient Oak Tree

I'm an ancient oak tree,
I am free.
I'm an ancient oak tree,
People saved me!
I was shielded by a person's truck,
He said to the bad people, "Bad luck!"
Please don't cut me down!
I love to be free!
Squirrels live in my crown!
I'm a home for the bee.

Patrick Trainor (6)
St Joseph's RC Primary School, London

Leaves

There is something brown that falls.
There's something that changes in seasons.
Something that is up high in a tree.
What could it be?
A nut or an acorn?
But also different sizes
Higher and higher,
But don't be a liar!
Shout out to the east and west,
Leaves are the best!

Elena Guinea (7)
St Joseph's RC Primary School, London

My Dream

We all need to be smart
We all need to do our part
From mountains to the sea
For every bird and every bee
For every colour of every fish
I have only just one wish
For everything that is small
To everything that is not at all
To make the planet clean
That would be my dream.

Phoebe Spiteri Hammer (6)
St Joseph's RC Primary School, London

Save The Earth

Save the Earth,
Save the trees,
Breathing around you,
Giving you life.

Save the Earth,
Save the plants,
Growing around you,
Giving us joy.

Save the Earth,
Save the nature,
Living around you,
Giving us a world to enjoy!
Save the Earth!

Anna Rizzato (10)
St Joseph's RC Primary School, London

The Animals Breathe

The air we breathe
The leaves will fly
The wind will grow
And sounds of animals you will hear
You will feel the wind in your ear
The air will breathe
A horse comes running to you
And a parrot too
You like it so much
You go again and never hurt animals again.

Mariana Sousa (8)
St Joseph's RC Primary School, London

The Ocean

The ocean is so deep and blue.
It's home to many fish,
Turtles and even whales too.

My home is clean and rubbish-free.
Why shouldn't these animals
Have homes like you and me?

The ocean is so deep and blue.
It shouldn't be home to plastic too.

Edie O'Brien (8)
St Joseph's RC Primary School, London

Nature

N one of you are helping me!
A recycling plan will save me
T all trees will help me
U se me kindly to survive and enjoy me
R ecycle and stop cutting trees, it will help me
E lectric cars will clean my air so that you can breathe.

Sophia Garrido Franco (8)
St Joseph's RC Primary School, London

Green Environment

Help the environment so we can live in peace
So the world does not cease
We need to get together and sow
In order for our plants to grow
Don't cut down trees
Protect the bees
So our flowers can pollinate
All pollution we should not tolerate.

Arabella Kojm Thompson (7)
St Joseph's RC Primary School, London

Big Earth

B lue planet
I really love you
G ood people take care of you

E normous job we have
A re you ready to be clean?
R ight, here we are
T o make you beautiful
H appy Earth, you will be with us!

Tita Mondedeu (6)
St Joseph's RC Primary School, London

How Useful Are Trees?

Trees are the most useful things.
If we did not have trees, what a poor thing!
Trees give us oxygen to breathe.
Imagine a world with no trees.
An Earth with no trees is a shame.
People would get sick and die, animals too.
Can you imagine?

Sesinna Zerezghi (7)
St Joseph's RC Primary School, London

Save The World

Do not chop a tree with birds and nests
Or the world will be a land of death.
The Amazon will not exist
When it becomes one little tree
So save the world
Please, please, please
So look after the trees.
Without a... *chop!*

Kai Man (10)
St Joseph's RC Primary School, London

Super World

World, world, rainy, windy, cosy in my home
World, world, snowy, sunny, cloudy in my holidays
World, world, I love jumping in puddles, *splash, splash*
World, world, I love kicking the leaves
World, world, you are my sweet home forever.

Ella Cali Gravier (7)
St Joseph's RC Primary School, London

The Amazon World

Sloths sliding on the trees
Dolphins diving in the water
Be happy, be sad
Be angry, be mad.

Sloths are calm, gentle, slow, sleepy
Dolphins are happy, hyper, bubbly, jumpy.

Come and see
All animals
With me...!

Cecilia Bailey (7)
St Joseph's RC Primary School, London

Cheetahs Are In Danger!

Cheetah's friends are rhinos and elephants
They are living less.
They used to eat the bushes,
Leaving the grass for cheetahs.
Now cheetahs are sad because the grass space is less.
Cheetahs are in danger but we are here to help.

Tomas Sanchez Roba (6)
St Joseph's RC Primary School, London

Nature Is The Best

N ature is the best
A nd we need to stop pollution
T o keep our animals, people and world safe
U se less plastic and stop polluting
R educe, reuse, recycle
E verything in our world matters.

Joel Fosu-Simpson (7)
St Joseph's RC Primary School, London

The Olive Tree

I am your olive tree
And apparently, I do not do anything
I do not move and I wish I could go to school like you
I heard your complaints
I clean the air
I give you olives
You protect me and I love you.

Isabella Lopez Alban (6)
St Joseph's RC Primary School, London

Our Planet

We love our planet
It lives and breathes around us
So let us keep it alive by...
Planting more trees!
Saving water!
Reusing and recycling!
Our planet loves us!
We need to love it back!

Christian Rafferty (6)
St Joseph's RC Primary School, London

Save Our Planet

I will turn the lights off and on when we need it.
I will turn the tap off and on when we need it.
Don't waste the paper.
Drawing just a dot.
Don't waste the food.
Eat the whole pot.

Leo Dallari (5)
St Joseph's RC Primary School, London

The Lights

If you want to save energy
What about turning the light off
Before going on a trip
Or turn your computer off
When you're not using it
So what do you think about these suggestions?

Ollie Henriot (7)
St Joseph's RC Primary School, London

Our Nature

N o more cutting down trees
A nd destroying our world
T ry to make a difference
U ndo deforestation
R ealise what you are doing
E nd this now!

Bella Pagnello Symmons (8)
St Joseph's RC Primary School, London

Summer

This is about seasons,
Autumn, spring, summer.
I'm a super summer lover,
I enjoy the sun.
I like the beach in Campoamor
I ride my bike singing this song.

Carmen Bianqui (6)
St Joseph's RC Primary School, London

Summer

I like summer at the beach
And I help to keep it clean
Taking plastic from the sea
Then I can relax with an ice cream.

Teresa Martin (5)
St Joseph's RC Primary School, London

Tree

I climb up the tree.
What a nice view of the sea!
I drink a cup of tea,
With the little honey bee!

Hans Lau (6)
St Joseph's RC Primary School, London

Global Warming

Oh heat, oh heat
No meat, no meat
We'll all be extinct
If we don't see they are linked!

Harry Leslie (7)
St Joseph's RC Primary School, London

Penguins

P enguins live in the Antarctic
E arth is getting warmer because of climate change
N othing can stop the penguins from sliding from the icy hills
G ood for their child that the mums catch food for them
U ntil we stop the littering, the Antarctic will be okay
I n the Antarctic, there are penguins and in the Arctic there are polar bears
N early all the world is heating up
S ave the penguins from climate change.

Maya Tworzydlo (8)
St Thomas' Primary School, Riddrie

The Arctic Fox

A rctic foxes live under bundles of snow.
R eally cold, they can't handle the snow.
C ould you handle the freezing weather?
T heir tails are a blanket for them to snuggle.
I n winter they are white but in summer, they turn brown.
C osy long ears like a really cosy soft blanket.

F oxes are nothing like Arctic foxes.
O ver the tall snowy hills they hunt.
X is for excellent little ears.

Lucy Graham (8)
St Thomas' Primary School, Riddrie

Arctic Fox

A rctic foxes are carnivores.
R eally long fluffy tails, acting like a blanket when curled up.
C ute when playing.
T heir fur is white and blends in with the snow.
I n warmer conditions, their fur changes colour to blend in.
C an they live in the Arctic? Yes they can.

F reezing cold temperatures.
O n days when the weather is harsh, they hibernate.
e **X** cellent sense of smell.

Xuxi He (9)
St Thomas' Primary School, Riddrie

Arctic Foxes

A rctic foxes are different than a fox.
R eally long tails like a cosy blanket.
C osy long ears like a fluffy pillow.
T hey eat polar bears' leftovers.
I n the warmer temperatures, their skin goes grey or blue.
C an they live in the Arctic?

F reezing cold temperatures.
O n their feet, they have fluffy fur.
X is for excellent hearing.

Tianna Baird (8)
St Thomas' Primary School, Riddrie

Polar Bears

P olar bears eat fish.
O n the Arctic, there are polar bears.
L ooking for food to eat.
A ntarctica has penguins.
R eally hard to swim so far.

B eing in the Arctic is hard because it is cold.
E very time polar bears need help.
A ntarctica is colder than the Arctic.
R eally hard to live there.
S o hard for animals to find food.

Jouri Alhamadani (8)
St Thomas' Primary School, Riddrie

Arctic Foxes

A rctic foxes are meat eaters
R odents are Arctic foxes' meals
C an you think of other Arctic animals?
T he Arctic is in the North
I know that Arctic foxes live in the Arctic
C old areas are where Arctic foxes live

F oxes are different from Arctic foxes
O nly Arctic foxes dive with their heads
X is for xtra-special foxes.

Milly Clelland (8)
St Thomas' Primary School, Riddrie

Arctic Foxes

A rctic foxes are meat eaters
R odents are Arctic foxes' meals
C old climates don't stop them
T emperatures are getting colder
I ce is getting slippier every day
C old gusts of snow

F oxes dig up seven holes into their homes
O n their tail, it is very furry and it is their blanket
X is for extraordinary hearing.

Louis Millican (9)
St Thomas' Primary School, Riddrie

Arctic Foxes

A rctic foxes eat meat.
R eally fluffy white tails.
C ould they survive in the Arctic?
T hat's something I'll never know.
I n the summer, it's still cold.
C ute when playing games.

F reezing temperatures.
O ver the hills they hunt.
X is for excellent hearing and smell.

Rebecca Winter (8)
St Thomas' Primary School, Riddrie

Polar Bears

P olar bears live in the Arctic.
O n the ice, they look for food.
L ooking for predators.
A ll the ice is melting.
R eally cold in the Arctic.

B aby polar bears stay with Mum.
E arth is warming up.
A ll the animals are suffering.
R eally hard survival
S ave our planet!

Macy Bannerman (8)
St Thomas' Primary School, Riddrie

Arctic Fox

A n Arctic fox is white
R eally don't like to swim
C ome and look at them
T oo hard to spot in the snow
I t is so cute, you can't stop
C ome to the Arctic fox party.

F un to watch them
O n the ice they wander
X -rays shows their bones are like cats' bones.

Aaron Murray (8)
St Thomas' Primary School, Riddrie

Arctic Fox

A rctic foxes are carnivores
R eally freezing cold, like an ice lake
C ould you go?
T hey tuck their tail in when they sleep
I n summer they go all brown
C an you live there?

F reezing temperature
O ver the hills, they trot over leaves
X is for excellent hearing.

Sienna Scott (8)
St Thomas' Primary School, Riddrie

Arctic Fox

A rctic foxes dig under snow
R eally colder than -58
C old and freezing
T he Arctic is cold
I t's so cold
C old -58 temperatures

F oxes dig underneath the snow
O n their feet is fluff
e **X** traordinary hearing.

Ryan McEwan (8)
St Thomas' Primary School, Riddrie

Arctic Foxes

A rctic foxes dig for prey
R ound little eyes
C osy when sleeping
T iny little paws
I n the warm, they turn brown
C arnivore is their type

F urry coat
O ver the hills they hunt
X is for extremely dangerous.

Aiden Cawley (8)
St Thomas' Primary School, Riddrie

Penguins

P enguins live in the Antarctic
E veryone help them!
N eed help with food
G ood belly sliders
U nable to live in hot countries
I n the Antarctic, penguins need lots of food
N eed our help
S ave the penguins.

Layla McConnell (8)
St Thomas' Primary School, Riddrie

Arctic Fox

A rctic foxes have big eyes
R ound little ears
C old weather
T emperatures are down
I ce is freezing
C ute eyes

F reezing temperatures
O n their feet, they have fur
e **X** cellent hearing.

Zac Brown (8)
St Thomas' Primary School, Riddrie

Arctic Foxes

A rctic foxes are cute!
R eally cold
C ute little ears
T hick coat of fat
I n the summer their hair goes brown
C arnivores

   F luffy tails
 l **O** ng coat
e **X** tremely cute.

Kirah O'Connor (8)
St Thomas' Primary School, Riddrie

The Arctic

A rctic is a blanket of snow
R eally freezing everywhere you go
C ould you survive there?
T hat's something I'll never know!
I cannot be able to live there!
'C ause the gusts of winds do blow!

Jessica Little (8)
St Thomas' Primary School, Riddrie

Arctic Foxes

Hi, I am the Arctic foxes
I go and hunt all alone
I build my dens wherever I go
There are seven entries around the place
And I have two kids
And I take them wherever I go.

Jessica Kane (8)
St Thomas' Primary School, Riddrie

YOUNG WRITERS INFORMATION

We hope you have enjoyed reading this book – and that you will continue to in the coming years.

If you're the parent or family member of an enthusiastic poet or story writer, do visit our website **www.youngwriters.co.uk/subscribe** and sign up to receive news, competitions, writing challenges and tips, activities and much, much more! There's lots to keep budding writers motivated!

If you would like to order further copies of this book, or any of our other titles, then please give us a call or order via your online account.

Young Writers
Remus House
Coltsfoot Drive
Peterborough
PE2 9BF
(01733) 890066
info@youngwriters.co.uk

Join in the conversation!
Tips, news, giveaways and much more!

YoungWritersUK YoungWritersCW youngwriterscw

Scan me to watch The Big Green video!